JAVA FOR BEGINNERS

An Introduction to Learn Java Programming with Tutorials and Hands-On Examples

Legal & Disclaimer

The information contained in this book and its contents is not designed to replace or take the place of any form of medical or professional advice; and is not meant to replace the need for independent medical, financial, legal or other professional advice or services, as may be required. The content and information in this book has been provided for educational and entertainment purposes only.

The content and information contained in this book has been compiled from sources deemed reliable, and it is accurate to the best of the Author's knowledge, information, and belief. However, the Author cannot guarantee its accuracy and validity and cannot be held liable for any errors and/or omissions. Further, changes are periodically made to this book as and when needed. Where appropriate and/or necessary, you must consult a professional (including but not limited to your doctor, attorney, financial advisor or such other professional advisor) before using any of the suggested remedies, techniques, or information in this book.

Upon using the contents and information contained in this book, you agree to hold harmless the Author from and against any damages, costs, and expenses, including any legal fees potentially resulting from the application of any of the information provided by this book. This disclaimer applies to any loss, damages or injury caused by the use and application, whether directly or indirectly, of any advice or information presented, whether for breach of contract, tort, negligence, personal injury, criminal intent, or under any other cause of action.

You agree to accept all risks of using the information presented in this book.

You agree that by continuing to read this book, where appropriate and/or necessary, you shall consult a professional (including but not limited to your doctor, attorney, or financial advisor or such other advisor as needed) before using any of the suggested remedies, techniques, or information in this book.

Table of Contents

1. Introduction

Java is a general purpose object oriented programming language. It follows ***"write once, run anywhere concept"*** which means Java code once compiled on one machine need not be re-compiled anywhere else and can potentially run off the shelf. This is possible because Java is designed to be a platform independent language.

In 1995, the first stable version of Java was released; originally developed by a Canadian computer scientist ***James Goslin*** while working at ***Sun Microsystems***. Sun Microsystems was acquired by ***Oracle Corporation*** in January 2010. Hence all Java trademarks are owned by ***Oracle Corporation*** at the time of writing this book.

1.1 Why Java?

Java is one of the most popular programming languages today with ever increasing demand in the IT industry. It is extremely popular and sometimes the most obvious choice for developing web applications and web services. There is a good chance that an average computer user comes in touch with technologies offered by or implemented using Java. In fact, some of the most common applications that we use on a day-to-day basis such as ***Gmail, ThinkFree Office, Minercraft, Vuze, etc***. are developed using Java either in part or completely.

Using Java, we can develop desktop applications, web applications, video games, mobile applications, etc. In fact, Android application development is primarily done using Java as it is the official android application development language alongside ***Kotlin***.

In order to learn Java, no prior programming experience is necessary but is advisable. Having the basic knowledge of C/C++ will help a great deal in learning Java. Having said that, you should be comfortable with using your system and shall have some experience in using Command Prompt on Windows and Terminal on Linux/MAC. If you are not comfortable with using Command Prompt/Terminal, it is a good idea to learn your way around these tools before beginning Java development.

1.2 Java Application Types

Although the Java framework keeps advancing, Java application types can be broadly classified into the following categories:

Desktop applications:

Desktop applications are designed for Windows, Linux and MAC. Can be a console based application that runs from a Command Prompt/Terminal or can have a GUI. These are also known as standalone applications.

Web applications/Web services:

Web applications/services are server side applications. Users normally interact with these applications using a browser.

Mobile/Embedded applications:

These are the applications that are meant for mobile or embedded devices.

2. Getting Started

In order to get started with Java development, you will have to install Java environment which consists of two distinct parts – ***Java Runtime Environment (JRE)*** which is used to run Java applications and ***Java Development Kit (JDK)*** which is used to compile Java source code in order to build applications. Installing JDK installs JRE automatically but installing JRE does not automatically install JDK. There are different Java editions available – ***Java SE (Standard Edition), Java EE (Enterprise Edition), Java ME (Micro Edition), etc.***

Java SE is the basic edition and is used to develop applications for desktops and servers. Java EE is used to extend the functionality of Java SE and develop web applications, web services and potentially cloud computing applications. Java ME is used to develop applications for mobile and embedded devices. In this book, we will be using Java SE and learn to develop basic desktop console applications. Applications can be developed on Windows, Linux and MAC. We will be using a Windows PC to do so. Java programs/source codes can be written using any text editor and carry the extension ***.java.***

2.1 Working of Java Programs

A Java program is compiled using a compiler which is a part of ***JDK.*** After successful compilation, ***platform-independent bytecode*** is generated. This bytecode is executed by ***Java Virtual Machine (JVM)*** which is a part of ***JRE.*** As long as the ***JVM*** is present on a device, the generated bytecode can be executed regardless of the computer architecture. This is a major advantage of Java. You can write a Java program and compile it on Windows, take the generated bytecode to MAC and execute it over there and anywhere else where JRE/JVM is present. In case of native programming languages such as C and C++, ***platform-specific machine level executable code*** is generated and is executed by the platform itself. A C++ program compiled in Windows cannot be executed off the shelf in MAC without recompiling. Whereas Java saves you the trouble of recompilation. The only downside is, since the bytecode is not native to a particular platform, it needs to be executed in a virtualized environment (taken care by JRE/JVM). This impacts the speed of execution and is not suitable for developing performance critical applications. Given the kind of powerful hardware that is available today, you will almost never encounter the speed issue.

2.2 Environment Setup

The default Java compiler is ***javac*** which is a part of JDK. In order to write Java programs, any text editor will do the job including ***Notepad***. I recommend a text editor called ***Notepad++*** (https://notepad-plus-plus.org/).

2.2.1 Installing Java Development Kit (JDK) on Windows

In order to install JDK on Windows, you will have to download JDK from Oracle's website – http://www.oracle.com/technetwork/java/javase/downloads/index.html. At the time of writing this book, the latest Java version is ***10.0.1***. The download location and version may change as time goes by. An appropriate web search should lead you to the correct download page and you should always download the latest version.

Once downloaded, execute the file to start the installation procedure. You may need administrative rights to do so. The installation Window should look like this:

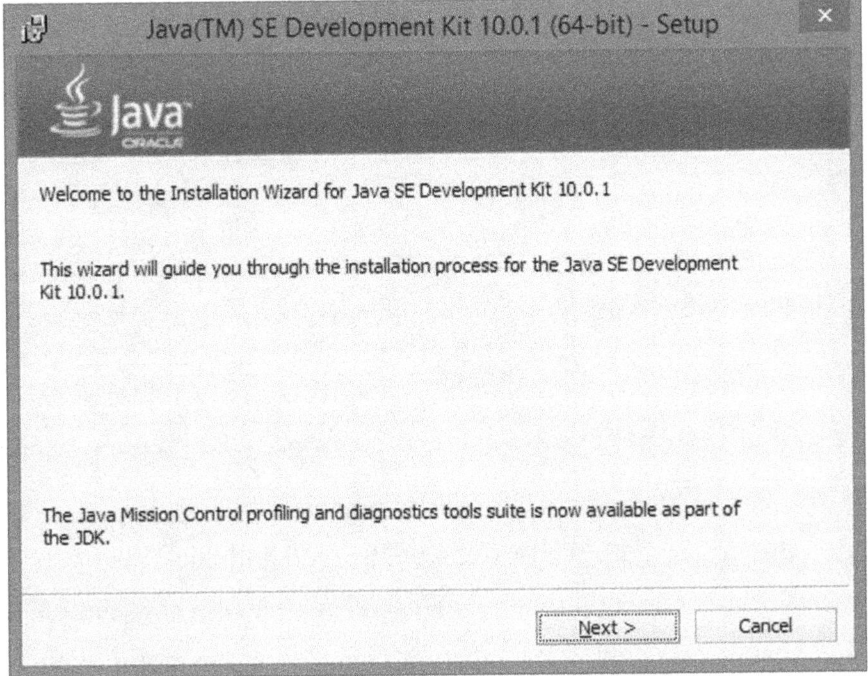

Click ***Next*** and the following window should appear:

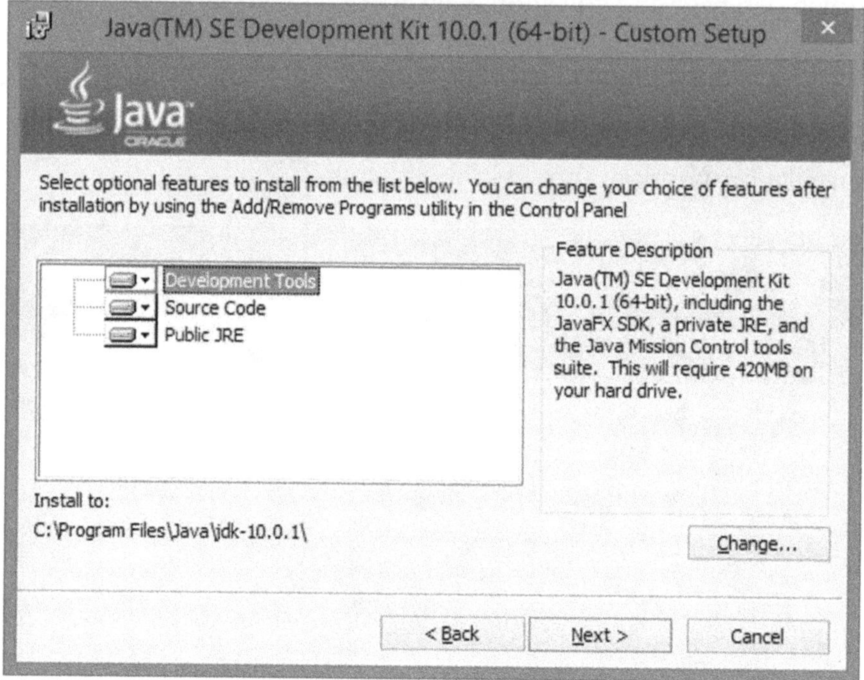

Here, you are given options to customize the installation. It is advisable to leave all the options unchanged and click ***Next***. The installation process will now begin and may take a few minutes. JRE installation will automatically begin at some point with a window similar to this:

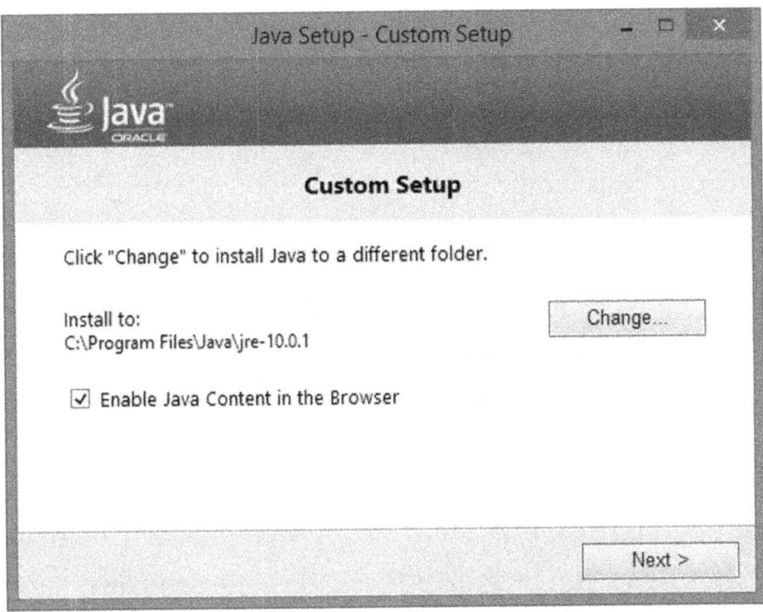

Leave the options unchanged and click ***Next***. This may take a few minutes. Once the installation is complete, you will see a window which will look like this:

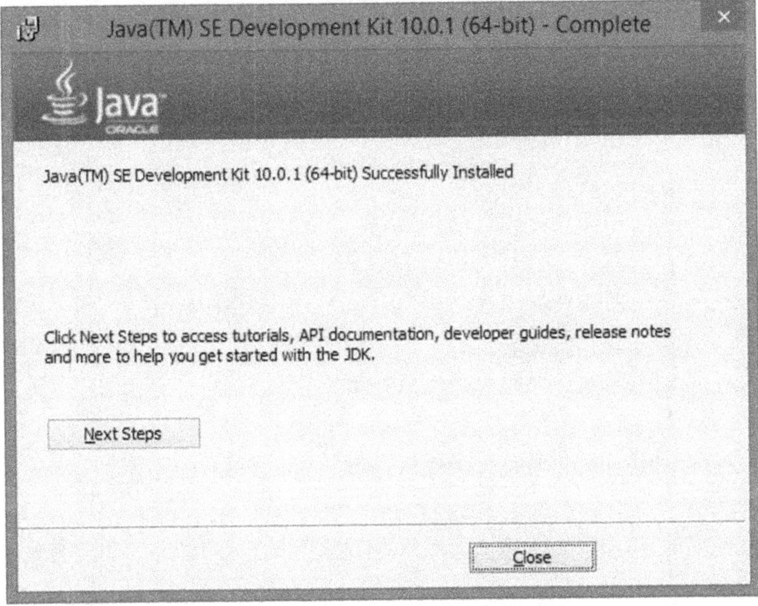

Note: This installation procedure is for Java version 10.0.1. The procedure usually does not change with changing versions but in case it varies slightly, read the description and follow the instructions thoroughly.

Once JDK and JRE is installed on the system, the Environment Variable ***Path*** needs to be set so that JDK can be accessed system wide including via Command Prompt. To do this, follow these instructions:

<u>**Step 1:**</u> Right click on ***My Computer/This PC***, click Properties. This opens ***System Properties***. You can alternatively press ***Windows Key + Pause Break*** on your keyboard.

<u>**Step 2:**</u> Click ***Advanced system settings*** on the left hand side and the following window should open.

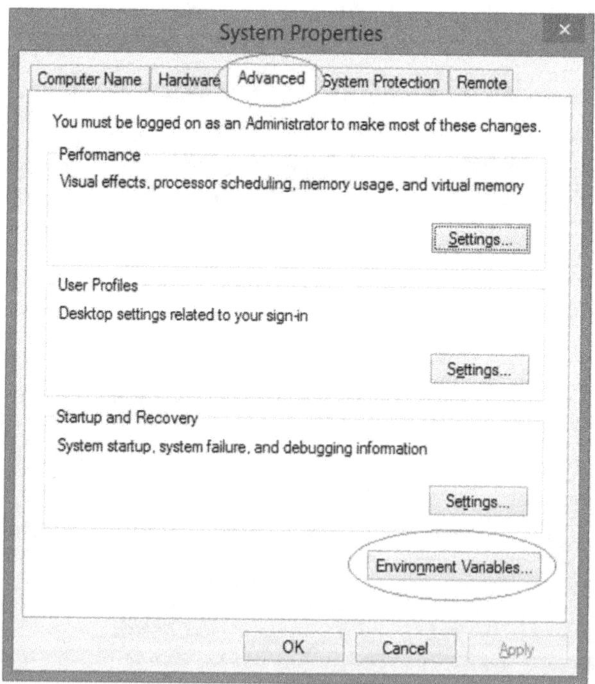

Step 3: Click Environment Variables, locate a variable called ***Path*** under ***System variables***. Select it and click ***Edit***.

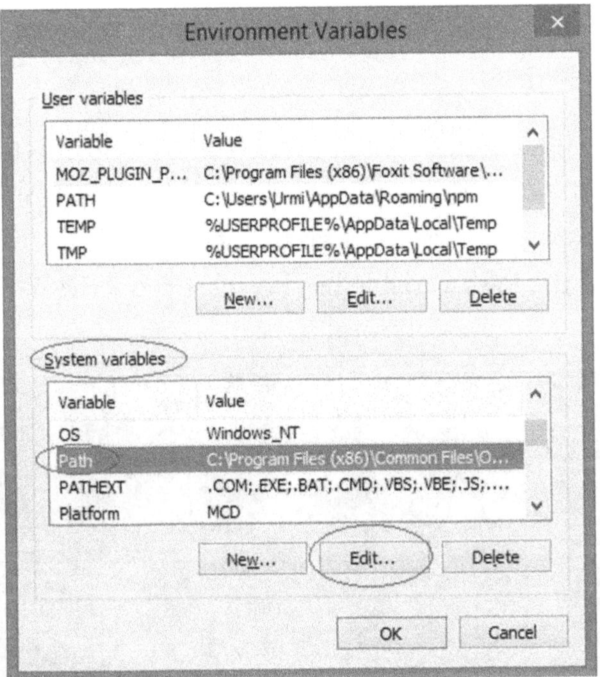

Step 4: Append a semi-colon (;) at the end of the contents of the ***Variable value*** field and add the full path of the ***bin*** folder which is present inside your ***JDK installation***. If you did not change any options during installation, it will most likely be ***C:\Program Files\Java\jdk-10.0.1\bin***. However, locate your JDK installation folder to be sure.

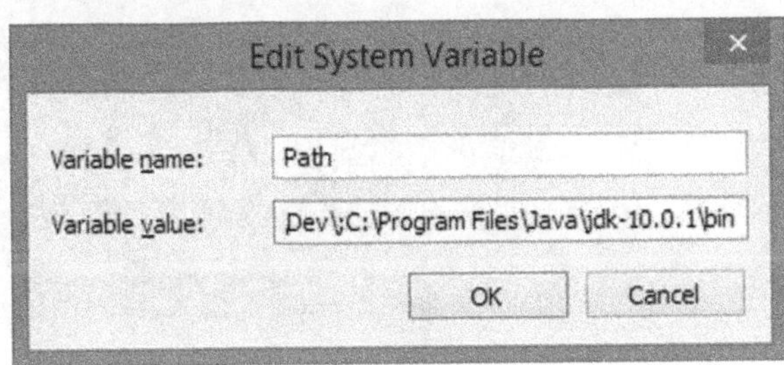

Click Ok and close all the open System Properties boxes by clicking Ok.

<u>**Note:**</u> You need Administrative rights in order to change System Properties.

Open Command Prompt, type ***javac*** and hit Enter; next, type ***java*** and hit Enter. If you see something like what is shown in the following two windows, Congratulations! Your JDK installation is perfect and the Path variable has been set properly!

```
CMD
F:\Java>javac
Usage: javac <options> <source files>
where possible options include:
  @<filename>                  Read options and filenames from file
  -Akey[=value]                Options to pass to annotation processors
  --add-modules <module>(,<module>)*
        Root modules to resolve in addition to the initial modules, or all modul
es
        on the module path if <module> is ALL-MODULE-PATH.
  --boot-class-path <path>, -bootclasspath <path>
        Override location of bootstrap class files
  --class-path <path>, -classpath <path>, -cp <path>
        Specify where to find user class files and annotation processors
  -d <directory>               Specify where to place generated class files
  -deprecation
        Output source locations where deprecated APIs are used
  -encoding <encoding>         Specify character encoding used by source files
  -endorseddirs <dirs>         Override location of endorsed standards path
  -extdirs <dirs>              Override location of installed extensions
  -g                           Generate all debugging info
  -g:{lines,vars,source}       Generate only some debugging info
  -g:none                      Generate no debugging info
  -h <directory>
        Specify where to place generated native header files
```

javac

```
CMD
F:\Java>java
Usage: java [options] <mainclass> [args...]
           (to execute a class)
   or  java [options] -jar <jarfile> [args...]
           (to execute a jar file)
   or  java [options] -m <module>[/<mainclass>] [args...]
       java [options] --module <module>[/<mainclass>] [args...]
           (to execute the main class in a module)

Arguments following the main class, -jar <jarfile>, -m or --module
<module>/<mainclass> are passed as the arguments to main class.

where options include:

    -cp <class search path of directories and zip/jar files>
    -classpath <class search path of directories and zip/jar files>
    --class-path <class search path of directories and zip/jar files>
                  A ; separated list of directories, JAR archives,
                  and ZIP archives to search for class files.
    -p <module path>
    --module-path <module path>...
                  A ; separated list of directories, each directory
                  is a directory of modules.
    --upgrade-module-path <module path>...
```

java

If you see an error which is something like this – 'javac' is not recognized as an internal or external command, operable program or batch file. **OR** 'java' is not recognized as an internal or external command, operable program or batch file, there is a problem either with JDK/JRE installation or with the Path variable. In such a case, follow steps given in **Section 2.2.1** again.

2.2.2 Installing Java Development Kit (JDK) on Linux and MAC OS X

Procedure to install JDK on a Linux OS varies from distro to distro.

For ***Debian/Ubuntu*** based distros, open ***Terminal*** and enter the following commands:

```
$> sudo apt-get update
$> sudo apt-get install default-jre
$> sudo apt-get install default-jdk
```

For any other Linux distro or MAC OS X, download the latest JDK from:

http://www.oracle.com/technetwork/java/javase/downloads/index.html and follow the instructions given at: https://docs.oracle.com/javase/9/install/installation-jdk-and-jre-linux-platforms.htm and https://docs.oracle.com/javase/10/install/installation-jdk-and-jre-macos.htm.

2.3 Optional IDE (Integrated Development Environment) Setup

An IDE is a software that offers tools to develop, compile, build, test, debug and package applications all under one roof. I do not recommend the usage of IDEs for beginners, not because of the ease they provide or because of the difficulties they may pose but because beginners should start from the basics and follow the bottom-up approach when learning a new programming language. Once you are comfortable with the basics of Java and know your way around, you may download and install an IDE and try working with it. Some of the best IDEs for Java are:

- Eclipse - https://www.eclipse.org/
- NetBeans - https://netbeans.org/
- IntelliJ IDEA - https://www.jetbrains.com/idea/

2.4 Program Compilation and Execution

We can write java programs in any text editor. A java program file should be saved with ***.java*** extension. To compile a java program, open Command Prompt and use the following command:

```
javac <Source File>.java
Eg:
javac FirstProgram.java
```

If the compilation is successful, a ***.class*** file having the same base file name as the source file will be generated. This file contains the machine independent bytecode that we discussed in ***Section 2.1***.

For example, if your source file was named ***FirstProgram.java***, upon successful compilation ***FirstProgram.class*** will be generated. Once the .class file is generated, you can execute your application with the following command:

```
java <Base Name of .class File>
Eg:
java FirstProgram
```

Note 1: For compilation, we use ***javac*** command and for execution we use ***java*** command. As a beginner, you can get confused between these two commands. Just remember that the 'c' at the end of ***javac*** command stands for 'compile'. We can execute a java application only after successful compilation and we should only specify the base file name of the .class file (without the extension) during execution.

Note 2: Compilation and execution procedure of java programs is the same across Windows, Linux and MAC. While we use Command Prompt in Windows, we user Terminal/Shell in Linux and MAC.

2.5 First Program

Let us put whatever we have learned in the previous section to use by taking an example. In this section, we will write a java program, compile and execute it. Open a text editor of your choice, copy-paste the following code and save the file as ***FirstProgram.java***

```
public class FirstProgram
{
    public static void main(String[] args)
    {
            System.out.println("This is my first Java program!!!");
    }
}
```

You do not have to understand the code as of now; you will learn to write java programs through the course of this book. Once saved, open ***Command Prompt*** on Windows or ***Terminal*** on Linux/MAC, navigate using the ***cd command*** to the directory where you saved this program. Compile the program with this command – ***javac Firstprogram.java.*** Execute the program with this command – ***java FirstProgram*** . Here is what the output will look like:

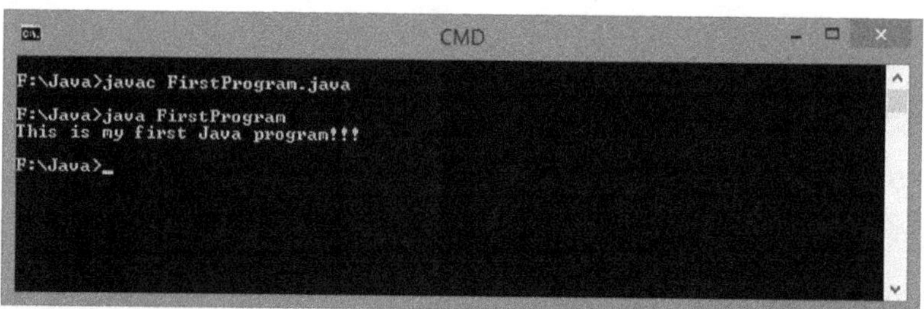

Here is the compilation and execution example for Linux /MAC using a Terminal:

You may cross-check the presence of ***FirstProgram.class*** file for your reference using the ***dir command*** in Windows Command Prompt or using the ***ls command*** in Linux/MAC:

CMD

```
F:\Java>dir
 Volume in drive F is Data
 Volume Serial Number is

 Directory of F:\Java

26-07-2018  11:28    <DIR>          .
26-07-2018  11:28    <DIR>          ..
26-07-2018  11:22               450 FirstProgram.class
26-07-2018  11:21               160 FirstProgram.java
               2 File(s)            610 bytes
               2 Dir(s)  166,209,974,272 bytes free

F:\Java>
```

<u>VERY IMPORTANT NOTE:</u> So far, we have learned how to set up java environment on a system and how to compile and execute java programs. Over the course of this book, we will write many java programs and hence you should be very comfortable with using the Command Prompt/Terminal and compilation/ execution of java programs.

3. Syntax

In this section, we will learn about the basic syntax of Java and also learn to write a simple Hello World program step by step. Java is a case sensitive language, which means "Chad" and "chad" are two different things.

3.1 Statements

A statement in Java is used to carry out a particular operation; be it logical, arithmetic, or any other computational operation. Each statement ends with a semicolon (;). You can write as many statements on one line by separating each one of them with a semicolon but this approach is not recommended as the code will look quite messy and discourage code readability. It is always good to have one statement on one line. Some examples of valid statements are as follows:

```
int x, y, z;
float pi = 3.14;
System.out.println("Java is awesome!");
```

3.2 Code Blocks

A block of code is a collection of statements enclosed within curly brackets ({ }). An example of a code block is demonstrated below:

```
{
    int a = 25;
    System.out.println("This is a block.");
}
```

Blocks are used extensively when working with classes, control structures and functions. You will learn more about these in the sections to follow.

3.3 Comments

Comments are ignored by the compiler and does not affect the code or the operation of the program in any way. Usually, people include comments in their codes to explain or mark a certain section of code. This book uses comments in codes extensively for explanatory purpose. Java offers single line comments and multi-line comments.

3.3.1 Single line Comments

A single line comment starts with a ***forward double-slash (//)***. Example:

```
//This is a single line comment.
//This is another comment.
```

3.3.2 Multi-line Comments

Multi-line comments are a group of comments that span over multiple lines. This group must be enclosed within ***forward slash asterisk (/*)*** and ***asterisk forward slash (*/)***. Example:

```
/* Multiline comment group starts here
You can have as many lines in between
...
...
*/
```

3.4 Identifiers

Identifiers are used to identify variables, functions, classes, objects, etc. Identifier names can contain alphabets (a-z, A-Z), numbers (0 – 9) and underscore (_). Since Java is a case sensitive language, the identifiers ***firstname*** and ***FirstName*** will be two different identifiers although they may mean the same thing logically. An identifier name can start with an alphabet or an underscore but cannot start with a number.

3.5 Keywords

Keywords in Java are reserved words which cannot be used as identifier names. Keywords have a specific meaning which tells the program what to do. Here is a list of them in alphabetical order:

abstract	assert	boolean	break
byte	case	catch	char
class	const	continue	default
do	double	else	enum
extends	final	finally	float
for	goto	if	implements
import	instanceof	int	interface
long	native	new	package
private	protected	public	return
short	static	strictfp	super
switch	synchronized	this	throw
throws	transient	try	void
volatile	while		

3.6 Introduction to Classes and Objects

Classes and Objects are a part of Object Oriented Programming (OOP) concepts. The OOP domain is huge and beyond the scope of this book. However, the basics will be covered in this sections because Java is a strictly object oriented language.

A ***class*** is a definition of a custom data type which is a collection of ***variables*** known as ***data members*** and ***functions*** that operate on these data members known as ***member functions.*** A class may or may not contain any data in itself and usually a mere definition of the data format.

An ***object*** is an instance of a class which has its own set of ***data members*** and ***member functions*** as defined in the class. ***Data members*** are also referred to as ***Attributes.***

The concept of classes and objects can be understood in a better way with an example. Let us consider a class called ***Laptop.*** When you imagine a laptop, what kind of properties can you think of? Some of the very common features like manufacturer, model, processor, RAM, OS, HDD capacity, etc. come to our mind. These properties are the ***variables*** of the class (or ***data members***) and each instance of this class is a different laptop with its own set of properties (or ***attributes***) such as manufacturer, model, processor, etc. In this scenario, each laptop is an object of the class ***Laptop.*** Take a look at the following diagram:

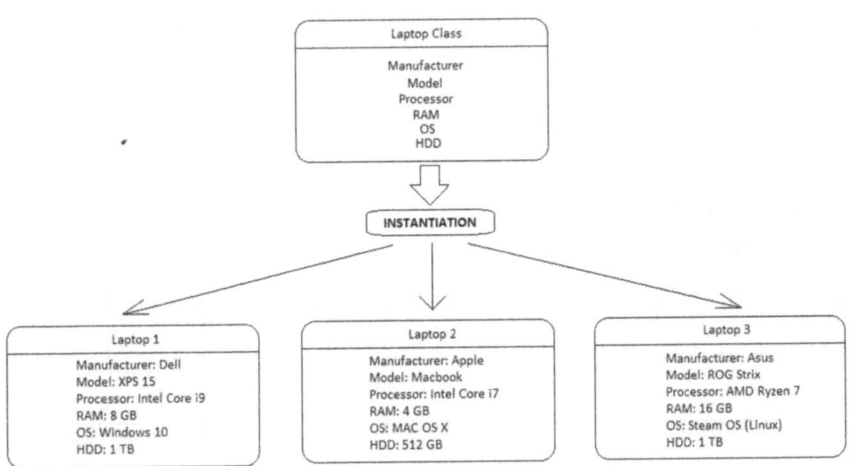

The above diagram shows the declaration of class Laptop which has the following data members: Manufacturer, Model, Processor, RAM, OS and HDD. Three instances of this class are created as objects. Each object is a different Laptop with its own set of data members.

In addition to classes and objects, here are a few more concepts you should know:

Instantiation: The process of creating an object.

Constructor: A special kind of a member function which has the same name as that of the class. It gets invoked automatically when an object is created.

Static members: Data members and member functions which are common for all objects. These are also known as class variables. When an object is created, it has its own set of data members as defined in the class except for static members.

Inheritance: A process of deriving a new class from an existing one thereby preserving some or all of the properties of the existing class.

Polymorphism: The ability to take more than one forms is called polymorphism. In Java, polymorphism can be seen in the form of function overloading and operator overloading. These are advanced OOP concepts and are not covered in this book.

Another important concept of OOP in Java that you should know about ***is access specifiers/access modifiers***. Access modifiers are used to set the accessibility or visibility of data members, member functions or classes. Java offers four access specifiers as follows:

private

Private members can be accessed only ***within the class*** and not from anywhere else.

default

When no access specifier is specified, it is default. Default members can be ***accessed within the same class and within the same package***.

protected

Protected members can be accessed ***within the class and package***. ***Using inheritance***, these members can be accessed from ***outside the package***.

public

Public members can be ***accessed from everywhere***, there are no restrictions.

Note: Data members and member functions can be public, private, protected or default but a class can either be default or public. The access specifiers private and protected cannot be used when declaring a class.

3.6.1 Accessing Data Members or Member functions

Data members and members can be accessed using the ***dot (.) operator***. General syntax:

```
<Object/Class/Package>.<Data Member/Member Function>
Eg:
Math.sqrt(4)
//Math is a class and sqrt is a static member
function of the Math class.
```

There could be nested classes or classes within a package. Hence you could see multiple dots in one statement.

3.7 Basic Java Program Structure

A basic standalone Java program must have the following constituents:

Package Statement

A package in Java is a group of classes. A package is identified by its name. You can give any name to a package. This is an optional statement. Once you start working on large Java projects, you will automatically feel the need to include this statement. General Syntax:

```
package <package name>;
Eg:
package xyz;
```

Once you use a package statement, all the classes in that program become a part of the mentioned package.

Import Statements

Import statements are used when you want to use classes from another package, either predefined or user-defined. General syntax:

```
import <package/package.class >;
Eg:
import java.lang.Math;
/* Here, java states that this is a built-in package
lang is the package and Math is a class that belongs
to the lang package
*/
```

The most common packages that you will import are ***java.io***, ***java.lang*** and ***java.util***. When you do not specify any import statement, ***java.lang*** is included by default implicitly. An asterisk (*) at the end of an import statement means import all the classes from that package. For example: ***import java.io.*;***

Class Definition

Since Java is a strictly object oriented language, classes are fundamental elements of Java programs. At least one class should be present in a program. There is no cap on the maximum number of classes, you can have as many as you want. Class definition is a block of code and hence it should be enclosed within curly brackets; it can contain data members, member functions, static members, etc. General Syntax:

```
<access specifier> class <Class Name>
    {
            //Statements…
            …
            …
    }
    Eg:
    class Student
    {
            String Name;
            int RollNumber;
    }
```

In the above example, ***no access specifier*** has been mentioned which means ***class Student*** is having a ***default*** access specifier. As we have seen in ***Section 3.6***, classes with a default access specifier can only be accessed within the same package. For a standalone program to work, the class should be accessible from anywhere. To do this, we need to make our class ***public*** as shown below:

```
public class Student
{
        String Name;
        int RollNumber;
}
```

Note: We will have only one class in all of our programs unless specified otherwise. This is to keep things simple and having multiple classes would mean we are digging deeper into OOP concepts which would complicate matters for beginners.

Main Method

The ***main method*** serves as an entry point to a ***standalone*** Java program. This is a mandatory component of a standalone Java program and should be part of the main class (the one that is declared as public). Without a main method, the program will not know where to start executing from. General Syntax:

```
public static void main (String [ ] args)
  {
        //Statements …
        …
        …
  }
```

String [ ] args is used for command line arguments. You do not need to know all about it, simply follow this template as a general syntax of the main method.

3.7.1 Rules of writing Java Programs

- There should be ***exactly one public class***; this is known as the ***main class*** of the program.
- The ***name of the source file*** should be the same as ***the name of the public class*** (main class) with ***.java*** as its extension. For example, if your main class is declared as ***public class Laptop***, the source file should be declared as ***Laptop.java***. This is very important; compilation will fail if the main class name and the source file name do not match.

- Every standalone program should have a ***mandatory main method*** as it is the entry point.
- If using package declaration, the package statement should be the first line of the code followed by the import statements. If no package declaration is used, the import statements should be the first lines.
- There is no limit on the presence of non-public classes, you can have as many as you want.

3.8 HelloWorld Application

Let us put to practice whatever we have learned in the previous section and write a simple standalone Java program to display a message on the console. What we did not learn is how to display something on the console which will be covered later in this section. Let us start with what we know so far:

Mandatory public main class:

We will name our public main class as ***HelloWorld.*** Keep in mind that this source file should be named as ***HelloWorld.java.*** Here is the code:

```
public class HelloWorld
{
}
```

Mandatory main method:

The mandatory main method should be present inside the main class as shown below:

```
public class HelloWorld
{
      public static void main (String [ ] args)
      {
      }
}
```

This is a good enough code for a standalone Java program. If you compile and execute it, it will work just fine but you will not see anything significant on the console as we are not doing anything to display anything on the console.

Writing to the console:

To write to the console, the following statement is used:

```
System.out.println ( <expression> );
```

System is a class which is a part of the ***java.lang*** package. ***out*** is an object of ***PrintWriter*** class which is indeed part of ***System*** class. ***println*** is a function defined in the ***PrintWriter*** class which is used to display text on a new line. ***<expression>*** could be anything from simple text (also known as ***constant string expression***), variables, constants or expressions. In order to display ***Hello World*** on the screen, we will specify text in the form of a constant string ***"Hello World"*** in place of ***<expression>***. Here's how the statement should look like:

```
System.out.println ( "Hello World" );
```

Alternatively, you can use the ***print*** function to write on the same line:

```
System.out.print ( "Hello World" );
```

You can use escape sequences such as **\n** and **\t** for new line and tab-space indent respectively. For example, the following statement will display ***Hello*** on one line and ***World*** on the next line:

```
System.out.println ( "Hello \nWorld" );
```

Multiple expressions can be combined in a ***println*** or ***print*** statement by inserting ***plus symbol (+)*** between expressions. This is actually the concatenation operator, used to combine more than one expressions in a string format. General Syntax:

```
System.out.println ( <expression 1> + <expression 2>
+ … <expression n> );
Eg:
//Will have the same output as System.out.println (
"Hello World" );
System.out.println ( "Hello" + " World" );
```

Putting everything together, we have the following code:

```
//Package statement would go here.

//Import statements (if any) would go here.
//No import statements needed for this program.

//Mandatory Main class definition (public class)
//Remember to name this file as HelloWorld.java


public class HelloWorld
{
    //Mandatory main method
    public static void main ( String [ ] args)
    {
            //println function displays text on the
screen
            System.out.println("Hello World");
    }
}
```

Now save this file as ***HelloWorld.java*** and open Terminal/ Command Prompt. Compile it as:

```
javac HelloWorld.java
```

Execute it as:

```
java HelloWorld
```

This is what the output would look like:

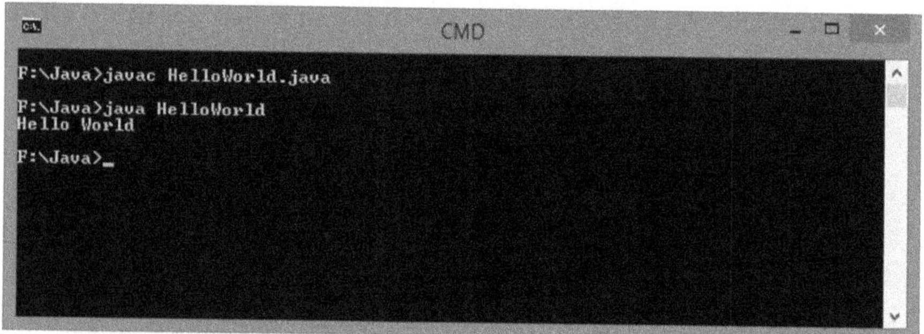

There is no package statement for the sake of simplicity. Import statements are not needed for this particular program as ***java.lang*** is implicitly included by default because of which we can use the ***System*** class (belonging to ***java.lang*** package).

If you have understood up to this point, Congratulations! You are on the right track to proceed and learn more about Java. If not, revise the previous chapters. This is a pivotal point; we have covered the fundamentals of writing a basic standalone Java program.

3.9 Compilation Errors

If you do not follow the syntax, semantics or rules of writing Java programs, the compiler will return an error when you run the

javac command. As a result, no ***.class*** file will be generated and you will not be able to execute your application.

Sometimes, the compiler will tell you what exactly has gone wrong where and sometimes the error message will be generic in nature. Let us take an example of a code which has a syntax error. Consider the ***HelloWorld*** example from the previous section and exclude a semicolon (;) at the end of the ***System.out.prinln*** statement on purpose to demonstrate compilation error:

THIS CODE IS WRONG, ONLY FOR DEMONSTRATION PURPOSE

```
public class HelloWorld
{
    //Mandatory main method
    public static void main ( String [ ] args)
    {
            //Do not terminate the following statement
with a semicolon
            System.out.println("Hello World")
    }
}
```

Here's what happened during compilation:

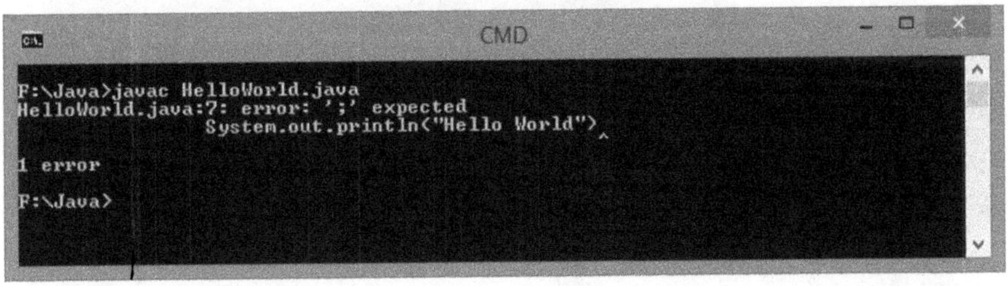

```
CMD
F:\Java>javac HelloWorld.java
HelloWorld.java:7: error: ';' expected
                System.out.println("Hello World")
                                                 ^
1 error

F:\Java>
```

In this case, the compiler informed us what has gone wrong and exactly where. Because compilation failed, ***HelloWorld.class*** file was not generated and hence ***java HelloWorld*** command could not find it as shown below:

```
CMD
F:\Java>dir
 Volume in drive F is Data
 Volume Serial Number is

 Directory of F:\Java

01-08-2018  10:25    <DIR>          .
01-08-2018  10:25    <DIR>          ..
01-08-2018  10:25               195 HelloWorld.java
               1 File(s)            195 bytes
               2 Dir(s)  164,497,387,520 bytes free

F:\Java>java HelloWorld
Error: Could not find or load main class HelloWorld
Caused by: java.lang.ClassNotFoundException: HelloWorld

F:\Java>_
```

We have stressed enough on the fact that the main class name should be the same as the source file name. Let us take another example where we will purposely name the source file different than the main class. Copy the correct and working HelloWorld application source code from ***Section 3.8*** and save it as ***ByeWorld.java***. Try to compile it as ***javac ByeWorld.java***. This is what you will see:

```
CMD
F:\Java>javac ByeWorld.java
ByeWorld.java:9: error: class HelloWorld is public, should be declared in a file
 named HelloWorld.java
public class HelloWorld
       ^
1 error

F:\Java>
```

In this case also, the compiler pointed out what is the problem and gave us the precise solution.

4. Data Types

Data types in Java are used to specify what kind of data we are dealing with. These are classified into two main categories – ***primitive data types*** and ***object/reference type data types***. You will come across various data types when dealing with variables, functions, type casting, type conversions, etc.

Here is a list of primitive data types:

Type	Description	Default	Size
boolean	Used to represent Boolean values of ***true*** or ***false***	false	1 bit
int	Signed integer, can range from -***2,147,483,648 to 2,147,483,647***	0	32 bits
short	Signed integer, can range from ***-32,768 to 32,767***	0	16 bits
long	Signed integer, used to represent large integer values; can range from -***9,223,372,036,854,775,808 to 9,223,372,036,854,775,807***	0	64 bits
float	Floating point; follows specification – ***IEEE 754***; can range from ***3.40282347 x*** $\boldsymbol{10^{38}}$ ***to 1.40239846 x*** $\boldsymbol{10^{-45}}$	0.0	32 bits
double	Floating point; follows specification – ***IEEE 754***; can range from ***1.7976931348623157 x*** $\boldsymbol{10^{308}}$ ***to 4.9406564584124654 x*** $\boldsymbol{10^{-324}}$	0.0	64 bits
byte	8-bit data type, can range from -***128 to 127 (or 0x00H to 0xFF in HEX)***	0	8 bits
char	Unicode character	\u0000	16 bits

Object/Reference data types are custom datatypes formed using object oriented concepts. One such data type that we will use is ***String*** which is used to store text data (or sequence of characters). String is actually a class defined inside ***java.lang*** package. We will use various data types throughout this book and concepts shall be clearer with examples.

5. Variables

A variable is a name given to a memory location. When a variable is declared, it is allotted some memory location that is accessible using a unique memory address. Remembering memory addresses is not an easy job. Hence most programming languages have a concept of variables. When declaring variables, we must specify its data type. In Java, the following syntax is followed to declare variables:

```
<data type> <variable name>;
Eg:
int x;
float f;
char c;
String name;
```

Multiple variables of the same data type can be declared on the same line as follows:

```
<data type> <variable 1>, <variable 1>, <variable 1>
…. <variable n>;
Eg:
int a, b, c;
String FirstName, LastName;
```

You can initialize a variable at the time of declaration using the equal-to (=) sign. The equal-to (=) sign is actually the ***assignment operator*** about which will learn in the ***Operators*** section in detail. For now, you just have to understand the basic function of this operator, that is – it is used to initialize/assign values to variables. General syntax for initialization is:

```
<data type> <variable name> = <initial value>;
Eg:
int x = 100;
boolean flag = true;
String FirstName = "Chad", LastName;
```

You can declare a variable anywhere in the program, and use them anywhere within the ***same code block after declaration***. You can use variables in expressions, change their values using assignment operator, display their contents, store user input (covered in **User Interaction** section), etc.

5.1 Constants

A constant is an identifier whose value cannot be changed. The value needs to be initialized at the time of declaration itself. It is technically a variable but calling a constant as a variable would be a misnomer because of obvious reasons. General Syntax:

```
final <data type> <variable> = <value>;
Eg:
final int number = 1256;
final double pi = 3.14, e = 2.7;
```

Below is a well commented Java program that uses variables. Some variables are initialized and some are assigned values later in the program. The values are displayed using ***System.out.prinln*** function:

```
//Mandatory public class
public class VariablesDemo
{
   //Mandatory main method
   public static void main ( String [] args )
```

```
    {
        //Declare int variables
        int a = 56, b;
        //Declare Boolean variables
        boolean yes = true, no ;
        //Declare double variables
        final double pi = 3.14 ;
        //Declare char variables
        char v = 'X';
        //Declare String
        String text;
        //Assign some non-initialized variables
        b = 825;
        text = "eBook";
        no = false;
        //Display Variables
        System.out.println("a = " + a + "\nb = " +
b );
        //println can display a mixture of variables
as long as the variable is displayable
        System.out.println("pi = " + pi + "\nv = "
+ v + "\ntext = " + text +
                                    "\nyes = " + yes +
"\nno = " + no);
    }
  }
```

Output:

```
CMD

F:\Java>javac VariablesDemo.java

F:\Java>java VariablesDemo
a = 56
b = 825
pi = 3.14
v = X
text = eBook
yes = true
no = false

F:\Java>
```

<u>Note 1:</u> When initializing/assigning variables of ***float*** type, the value should be suffixed with ***F*** and ***double*** values should be suffixed with ***D***, for example, ***float f = 4.56F; double d = 78.709D***. Double values will work without a ***D suffix*** but float values will not work without a ***F suffix***.

<u>Note 2:</u> You cannot assign non-compatible values to a variable of a different type. For example, you cannot say **int x = "eBook"**. Here, x is a variable of integer type while "eBook" is a string.

5.2 Basics of Defining Classes and Data Members

In this section, we will learn the absolute basics of defining classes, data members and accessing those data members. We already know that there can be only one public class (mandatory main class) and any number of non-public (default classes). To keep confusion at bay, I reiterate that the naming convention for the source file remains unchanged – filename should be the same as the public class name with ***.java*** as its extension. We have seen the basic syntax of class declaration, let us go through it again:

```
class <class name>
{
        //Data members..
        //Member functions..
        ...
        ...
}
```

In your source file, alongside the public class the code will look like this:

```
class <class name>
{
      //Data members..
      //Member functions..
      ...
      ...
}
public class <main class name>
{
      public static void main ( String [ ] args )
      {
            //Statements ...
      }
}
```

Each data member inside a class can either be public, private, default or protected. ***Public*** data members are accessible from everywhere; ***default*** data members are accessible from outside the class but within the same package. ***Private*** and ***protected*** data members cannot be accessed from outside the class directly and ***member functions*** of the same class are needed to do the same. The concept of member functions and playing with access specifiers requires proper understanding of object oriented programming concepts. Hence, we will only use ***default*** and/or ***public*** data members. Here is a template:

```
class <class name>
{
      public <data type> <variables>;
      <data type> <variables>;
      ...
}
```

You can initialize variables in the class declaration itself but cannot assign inside the class. For example, you can do this:

```
Class Demo
{
        int x = 100;
}
```

But you cannot do this:

```
Class Demo
{
        int x ;
        x = 100;
}
```

Class definition is a mere blueprint. Instance of the class must be created to access data members. ***Each instance*** is known as an ***object*** and each object has its own set of data members except for static data members which are common for all objects. Let us take an example of class definition:

```
class Person
{
    String name;
    int age;
    double weight;
    static int count;
}
```

We see a non-public (default) ***class Person*** with several data members. Since no access modifiers are mentioned, these data members will be treated as ***default*** which are accessible from outside the class but within the same package. When objects of ***class Person*** are created, each object will have its own set of

name, age and weight but not ***count*** as it has been declared as ***static***. To declare an object of a class, the following syntax is used:

```
<class name> <object name>;
```

This is mere declaration, not instantiation. ***Instantiation*** is done with the help of ***new*** keyword to allocate memory for objects and is mandatory. General Syntax:

```
<class name> <object name> = new <class name> ( );
```

You can declare an object first and later instantiate as follows:

```
<class name> <object name>;
<object name> = new <class name> ( );
```

Instantiation has to happen somewhere before you try to access the data members.

From the above ***class Person*** example, you can create objects (and initialize) as follows:

```
Person p = new Person ( );
```

Person () is actually a ***constructor***. A constructor is a member function that has the same name as that of the class. As seen from the class definition, we neither have declared any member functions nor any constructors. In such a case, a default constructor (not to be confused with the default access specifier) is implicitly made available. Once the object has been created and initialized, you can access the data members using the dot (.) operator as follows:

```
<object name> . <data member>
```

You can assign values as follows:

```
<object name>.<data member> = <value>;
```

For example, if you want to assign some value to the ***String name*** and ***int age*** data members of ***object p*** belonging to ***class Person*** (assuming that the object has been created and initialized), the following statements will be used:

```
p.name = "Tom";
p.age = 50;
```

Accessing static members can be done using the ***class name itself.*** For example:

```
Person.count = 1 ;
```

Let us put all this to practice and write a Java program that defines ***class Person*** alongside the main class, create and initialize objects of ***class Person*** and access them.

```
//Define class Person, this is not the main class
class Person
{
    //Declare data members
    String name;
    int age;
    double weight;
    //Declare static data member
    //This is accessed as Person.count
    static int count;
}
//Mandatory public main class
public class ClassDemo
{
    //Mandatory main method
    public static void main ( String [ ] args )
    {
```

```
        //Create and initialize object p1 of type
class Person
        Person p1 = new Person();
        //Set name of p1
        p1.name = "Maya";
        //Set age of p1
        p1.age = 25;
        //Set weight of p1
        p1.weight = 53.6;
        //Declare object p2 of type class Person
        Person p2;
        //Initialize p2 by instantiation using new
keyword
        p2 = new Person();
        //Set name of p2
        p2.name = "Samantha";
        //Set age of p2
        p2.age = 32;
        //Set weight of p2
        p2.weight = 63.1;
        //Set static member count of class Person
        Person.count = 2;
        //Display data member of p1
        System.out.println("\nData                of
p1\n================\nname: "
                                        + p1.name +
"\nage: " + p1.age + "\nweight: "
                                        + p1.weight +
"\n================");
        //Display data member of p2
        System.out.println("\nData                of
p2\n================\nname: "
                                        + p2.name +
"\nage: " + p2.age + "\nweight: "
                                        + p2.weight +
"\n================");
        //Display static data member count of class
Person
```

```
            System.out.println("\ncount:        "        +
Person.count );

      }
   }
```

Output:

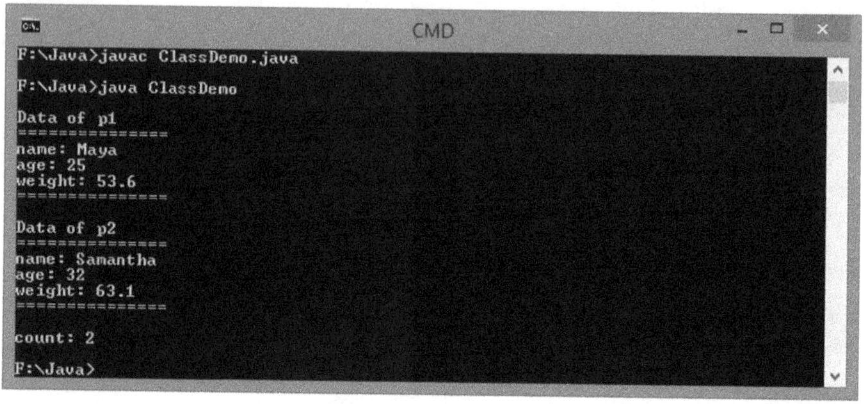

```
F:\Java>javac ClassDemo.java

F:\Java>java ClassDemo

Data of p1
==============
name: Maya
age: 25
weight: 53.6
==============

Data of p2
==============
name: Samantha
age: 32
weight: 63.1
==============

count: 2

F:\Java>
```

6. Operators

An operator in a programming language is a symbol that performs a computational task. Operators in Java are used to perform mathematical, logical or comparison operations. The following types of operators are available:

1. Arithmetic Operators
2. Logical Operators
3. Bitwise Operators
4. Relational Operators
5. Assignment Operators

6.1 Arithmetic Operators

Arithmetic operators are used to perform mathematical operations such as addition, subtraction, division, etc.

Operator	Description	Sample Usage	Explanation
+	Addition	x + y	Performs arithmetic addition, returns sum of the operands.
-	Subtraction	x - y	Performs arithmetic subtraction, returns difference of the operands.
*	Multiplication	x * y	Multiplies operands and returns the arithmetic product.
/	Division	x / y	Performs division and returns the arithmetic quotient.
%	Modulus	x % y	Performs division and returns the remainder. This operator can only be used on integer type operands.

++	Increment	x ++	Increments the value of an operand by 1. Two variations: Post increment (x ++) and Pre increment (++ x). This operator works only on integer variables.
--	Decrement	x --	Decrements the value of an operand by 1. Two variations: Post increment (x --) and Pre increment (-- x). This operator works only on integer variables.

Note: If you divide an integer by another integer, the quotient will be an integer even if the arithmetic value of the quotient should be a floating point value. For example, the quotient resulting from this division –> ***13 / 4*** will be ***3*** and not ***3.25***. To solve this, a float factor must be introduced. You can multiply 1.0 to either the numerator or the denominator. The expression ***13 / 4*** will now become ***13 * 1.0 / 4*** or ***13 / 4 * 1.0***. You can even use brackets just as you would in mathematics for convenience or when you want to carry out an operation first among an expression – > ***13 / (4 * 1.0)***.

```
eg:
int x = 13, y = 4;
float quotient = ( x * 1.0 ) / y;
```

6.2 Logical Operators

Logical operators are used to carry out logical AND, OR and NOT. These operators can only be used on Boolean operands or expressions and return a Boolean value of ***true*** or ***false***.

<table>
<tr><th>Operator</th><th>Description</th><th>Sample Usage</th><th>Explanation</th></tr>
<tr><td>&&</td><td>Logical AND</td><td>x && y</td><td>Compares operands and returns true if all the values are true, returns false otherwise.</td></tr>
<tr><td>||</td><td>Logical OR</td><td>x || y</td><td>Compares operands and returns true if any one of the values is true, returns false otherwise.</td></tr>
<tr><td>!</td><td>Logical NOT</td><td>!x</td><td>Returns inverted value of the operand. If the operand has a true value, false will be returned and if the operand has false value, true will be returned.</td></tr>
</table>

6.3 Bitwise Operators

Bitwise operators are used to perform bit-by-bit logical operation. That is, operations are carried out on each bit of the operands.

<table>
<tr><th>Operator</th><th>Description</th><th>Sample Usage</th><th>Explanation</th></tr>
<tr><td>&</td><td>Bitwise Logical AND</td><td>x & y</td><td>Performs logical AND on each of the operands on a bit-by-bit basis.</td></tr>
<tr><td>|</td><td>Bitwise Logical OR</td><td>x | y</td><td>Performs logical OR on each of the operands on a bit-by-bit basis.</td></tr>
<tr><td>~</td><td>Bitwise Logical Inverter</td><td>~x</td><td>Inverts each bit of the operand.</td></tr>
<tr><td>^</td><td>Bitwise Logical XOR</td><td>x ^ y</td><td>Performs logical XOR on each of the operands on a bit-by-bit basis.</td></tr>
<tr><td><<</td><td>Left Shift</td><td>x << y</td><td>Left shifts bits of the operand on the left by a number specified by the right operand. From Sample Usage, x << y will result in x's bits left shifted y times.</td></tr>
<tr><td>>></td><td>Right Shift</td><td>x >> y</td><td>Right shifts bits of the operand on the left by a number specified by the right operand. From Sample Usage, x >>y will result in x's bits right shifted y times.</td></tr>
</table>

6.4 Relational Operators

Relational Operators are used to compare the given operands. These operators return a Boolean value of either ***true*** or ***false***.

Operator	Description	Sample Usage	Explanation
==	Equal To	x == y	Returns ***true*** if the value of the operands is equal, ***false*** otherwise.
!=	Not Equal To	x != y	Returns ***true*** if the value of the operands is not equal, ***false*** otherwise.
<	Less Than	x < y	Returns ***true*** if the value of the left operand is less than the value of the operand on the right, ***false*** otherwise.
>	Greater Than	x > y	Returns ***true*** if the value of the left operand is greater than the value of the operand on the right, ***false*** otherwise.
<=	Less Than OR Equal To	x <= y	Returns ***true*** if the value of the left operand is less than OR equal to the value of the operand on the right, ***false*** otherwise.
>=	Greater Than OR Equal To	x >= y	Returns ***true*** if the value of the left operand is greater than OR equal to the value of the operand on the right, ***false*** otherwise.

6.5 Assignment Operators

The ***equal-to (=)*** sign is the de-facto assignment operator in Java and many other programming languages. It is used to assign values to variables. We have seen the basic usage of the assignment operator in ***Section 5***. In this section, we will discuss assignment operators in detail. General Syntax:

```
<operand 1> = <operand 2>
eg:
a = 965;
x = a * 2;
b = x;
```

Assignment operator, assigns the value of the operand on the right to the operand on the left. Operand on the left side of the assignment operator has to be a variable. Operand on the right side of the assignment operator can be a constant, variable or an expression. In case of an expression, it will be evaluated first and then the value will be assigned except when a post-increment/ decrement operator is used as demonstrated in the code snippet below:

```
int x = 45;
int y = x++;
```

The variable ***x*** has been initialized to ***45***. In the next statement we see ***int y = x++***. In this case, the value of ***x*** which is ***45*** will be assigned to ***y*** first and then ***x*** will be incremented. Now**,** ***x = 46 and y = 45***. If pre-increment operator was used, the value would have been incremented first and then assigned. If we had a statement ***int y = ++x***, then ***x*** would be incremented first and then assigned to ***y***. Hence, both ***x*** and ***y*** would hold the value ***46***.

Multiple variables can be assigned the same value as follows:

```
<variable 1> = <variable 2> = <variable 3> … <variable n> = <value>;
```

Eg:

```
int x, y, z;
x = y = z = 1500;
```

In this case, all 3 variables x, y and z will have a value of 1500.

6.5.1 Compound Assignment Operators

Compound Assignment Operators are used to perform mathematical operations on operands first and then assign.

<table>
<tr><th>Operator</th><th>Description</th><th>Sample Usage</th><th>Equivalent To</th></tr>
<tr><td>+=</td><td>Perform arithmetic addition, then assign</td><td>x += y</td><td>x = x + y</td></tr>
<tr><td>-=</td><td>Perform arithmetic subtraction, then assign</td><td>x -= y</td><td>x = x - y</td></tr>
<tr><td>*=</td><td>Perform arithmetic multiplication, then assign</td><td>x *= y</td><td>x = x * y</td></tr>
<tr><td>/=</td><td>Perform arithmetic division, then assign</td><td>x /= y</td><td>x = x / y</td></tr>
<tr><td>%=</td><td>Calculate modulus, then assign</td><td>x %= y</td><td>x = x % y</td></tr>
<tr><td>&=</td><td>Perform Bitwise Logical AND, then assign</td><td>x &= y</td><td>x = x & y</td></tr>
<tr><td>|=</td><td>Perform Bitwise Logical OR, then assign</td><td>x |= y</td><td>x = x | y</td></tr>
<tr><td>^=</td><td>Perform Bitwise Logical XOR, then assign</td><td>x ^= y</td><td>x = x ^ y</td></tr>
<tr><td><<=</td><td>Perform left shift, then assign</td><td>x <<= y</td><td>x = x << y</td></tr>
<tr><td>>>=</td><td>Perform right shift, then assign</td><td>x >>= y</td><td>x = x >> y</td></tr>
</table>

Here is a Java program that demonstrates the usage of various operators:

```
public class OperatorDemo
{
    public static void main ( String[] args )
    {
            //Declare some variables
            int number1 = 165, number2 = 5853, sum ;
            int x, y;
            float length = 26.365F, width = 132.968F,
area;
            double quotient, a = 63.568, b = 65897.0256;
            boolean bool1 = true, bool2 = false, r1, r2;
            //Arithmatic Operators
            sum = number1 + number2 ;
            area = length * width ;
            quotient = ( number1 / ( number2 * 1.0 ));
            //Logical Operators
            r1 = bool1 && bool2 ;
            r2 = bool1 || bool2 ;
            //Bitwise Operators
            x = number1 | number2 ;
            y = number1 ^ number2 ;
            //Compound Assgnment Operators
            b += a;
            //Display initialized values:
            System.out.println("\nnumber1 = " + number1
+
                                                "\nnumber2 =
" + number2 +
                                                "\nlength = "
+ length +
                                                "\nwidth = "
+ width +
                                                "\na = " + a
+
                                                "\nb = " + b
+
                                                "\nbool1 = "
+ bool1 +
                                                "\nbool2 = "
+ bool2);
            //Display computed values
            System.out.println("\n\nsum = " + sum +
```

```
                                        "\narea = " +
area +
                                        "\nquotient =
" + quotient +
                                        "\nr1 = " + r1
+
                                        "\nr2 = " + r2
+
                                        "\nx = " + x
+
                                        "\ny = " + y
+
                                        "\nb = " + b);
        }
    }
```

Output:

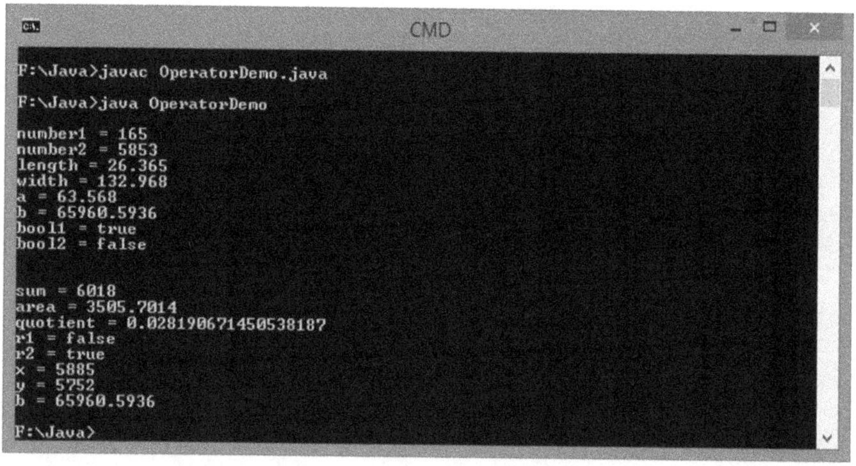

```
CMD
F:\Java>javac OperatorDemo.java

F:\Java>java OperatorDemo

number1 = 165
number2 = 5853
length = 26.365
width = 132.968
a = 63.568
b = 65960.5936
bool1 = true
bool2 = false


sum = 6018
area = 3505.7014
quotient = 0.028190671450538187
r1 = false
r2 = true
x = 5885
y = 5752
b = 65960.5936

F:\Java>
```

Note: Java supports ***Operator Overloading*** with which one operator can be used for multiple purposes. For example, the plus symbol (+) can be used to add two numeric values as well as to concatenate two strings. Operator Overloading is an advanced OOP concept and is not covered in this book.

7. User Interaction

So far, whatever concepts we have learned did not have any sort of user interaction with the applications. Programs were written with hardcoded values and operations were performed. In this section, we will learn how to accept user input and store it in variables. There are multiple ways to read user inputs – using ***BufferedReader class (java.io. BufferedReader), Scanner class (java.util.Scanner) and Console class (java.lang.System).*** Out of these, we will learn how to accept user input using the ***Scanner class*** as it is the easiest one to learn and the best for beginners. In order to make use of this class, you need to include ***java.util.Scanner*** in your program. This is done using the ***import*** keyword (covered in ***Section 3.7***) as follows:

```
import java.util.Scanner;
      OR
Import java.util.*;
```

A good thing about ***Scanner class*** is that it provides different functions for reading inputs of different data types. Following are the available functions:

Function	**Description**
public String ***next()***	Reads user inputs and returns the value as ***String.***
public String ***nextLine()***	In a multi-line input, next line is read and returned as ***String.***
public byte ***nextByte()***	Reads the input and returns a ***Byte.***
public short ***nextShort()***	Reads the input and returns a ***short integer.***
public int ***nextInt()***	Reads the input and returns an ***integer.***

public long ***nextLong()***	Reads the input and returns a ***long integer.***
public float ***nextFloat()***	Reads the input and returns a ***float value.***
public double ***nextDouble()***	Reads the input and returns a ***double value.***

First, an ***object*** of ***Scanner class*** needs to be created and initialized using the following syntax:

Scanner scanobj = new Scanner (System.in);
//scanobj is the object name, could be anything. Follow variable naming rules.

The functions mentioned in the above table return a value of a particular data type. A variable of the same data type is needed to store the returned value. We will study how functions work, what are return types, etc. in detail in ***Functions*** section. For now, you only have to understand how to use functions of the Scanner class.

After an object of Scanner class is declared and initialized (let us call it ***scanobj*** from here on out of convenience), the following syntax is used to read user input:

```
<variable> = scanobj.<Scanner class function>;
Eg:
//For reading String values:
String s = scanobj.nextLine ( );
//For reading integers:
int number = scanobj.nextInt ( );
//For reading floating point values:
float f = scanobj.nextFloat ( );
//For reading Double values
double d = scanobj.nextDouble ( );
```

The input function ***nextLine ( )*** is a better choice to read strings over ***next ( )*** because when we enter a string and hit enter, next line character ***\n*** is appended at the end.

When reading input from the user, you should be careful with the data type. If you are asking the user to enter an integer, using ***scanobj.nextInt ( )*** to read the input as an integer and the user enters a string then it will cause a runtime error known as an ***exception***. Exception handling is a fairly advanced topic and is beyond the scope of this book.

Note: All of these functions implement ***blocking I/O operations***. This means, when the program execution encounters one of these functions, the program will halt execution and wait for user to enter something on the console.

Here is a program that uses Scanner class in order to read various inputs:

```
   //Needed to use the java.util.Scanner class
   //Without this, you will not be able to access Scanner
class

   import java.util.*;

   //Mandatory public class

   public class UserInput
   {

       //Mandatory main method

       public static void main ( String [] args )
       {
              //Declare variables
              int zipcode;
              float temperature;
              String city;
```

```
            //Declare  and  initialize  Scanner  object
scanobj
            Scanner scanobj = new Scanner( System.in );
            //Ask the user to enter a city
            System.out.println("\nEnter City: ");
            //Read user input in string form
            city = scanobj.nextLine();
            //Ask the user to enter Zipcode
            System.out.println("\nEnter Zipcode: ");
            //Read user input in int form
            zipcode = scanobj.nextInt();
            //Ask the user to enter temperature
            System.out.println("\nEnter    Temperature:
");
            //Read user input in float form
            temperature = scanobj.nextFloat();
            //Display everything
            System.out.println("\n\nCity: " + city +
                                          "\nZipcode: "
+ zipcode +

      "\nTemperature: " + temperature + " F");
      }
   }
```

Output

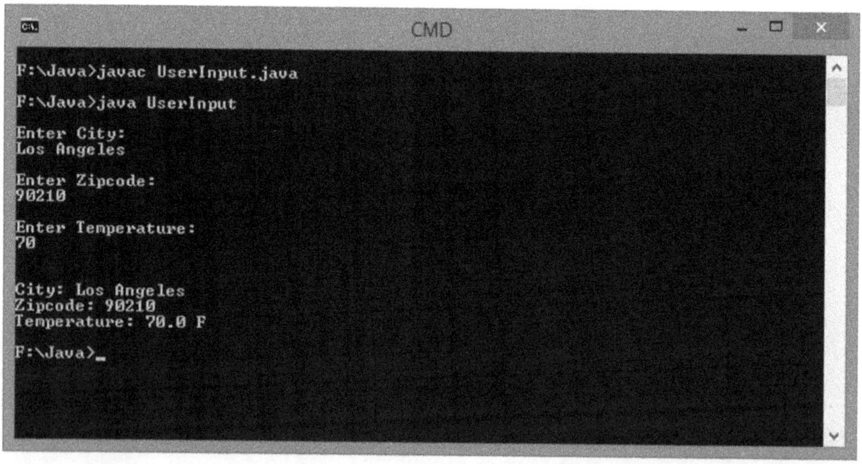

```
F:\Java>javac UserInput.java

F:\Java>java UserInput

Enter City:
Los Angeles

Enter Zipcode:
90210

Enter Temperature:
70


City: Los Angeles
Zipcode: 90210
Temperature: 70.0 F

F:\Java>_
```

8. Control Structures

Control structures are used to exercise control over the execution of a program. Normally, a program would go about executing statements sequentially but there may arise a situation where we do not want a sequential execution. This is accomplished with the help of control structures. Java offers control structures in the form of ***decision making*** and ***loops***. We will take a look at each one of them.

8.1 Decision making

Decision making constructs are available in the form of ***if-else*** and ***switch*** statements.

8.1.1 if-else

The if-else construct is used where you come across – "if this happens, then do something; otherwise do something else".

The general syntax for using an **if** statement is as follows:

```
if ( <condition> )
{
        //This is the if-block
        <statements…>
}
```

Once the program execution reaches the ***if*** statement, the expression in the ***<condition>*** field is evaluated. The ***<condition>*** has to be a Boolean expression which can either evaluate to a Boolean value of ***true*** or ***false***. If the evaluation returns ***true***, statements inside the ***if-block*** are executed, a ***false*** value will skip the execution of the ***if-block***. A block is enclosed within curly brackets ({ }). The ***if-block*** can be optionally followed by a corresponding ***else-block*** as follows:

```
if ( <condition> )
{
        //This is the if-block
        <statements...>
}
else
{
        //This is the else-block
        <statements...>
}
```

When there are ***if*** and ***else*** blocks and the specified condition of the ***if statement*** evaluates to ***false***, only then the following ***else-block*** will be executed.

Note: If you plan to include an ***else*** block, it should immediately follow the ***if*** block. There should not be any statements between the closure of ***if*** block and before the start of the corresponding ***else*** block.

Nesting of ***if-else*** statements is allowed. The rules are the same as that of any other ***if-else*** construct. Here is an example:

```
if ( <condition 1>)
        {
        //This block will be executed if <condition 1> is
true.
        if ( <condition 2> )
                {
```

```
    //This block will be executed if <condition 1> and
    <condition 2> is true.
            <statements…>
    }
    else
    {
            //This block will be executed if <condition
            1> is true and <condition 2> is false.
                    <statements…>
            }
    }
    else
    {
            //This block will be executed if <condition
1> is false.
            if ( <condition 3> )
            {
            //This block will be executed if <condition
            1> is false and <condition 3> is true.
                    <statements…>
            }
    }
```

Another way to write multiple ***if-else*** statements is using the ***else if*** construct. The way ***else if*** construct work is – There will be a mandatory ***if*** statement, if the condition of the ***if*** statement evaluates to ***false***, the control will go to the immediate ***else if*** statement (if it is present) and will evaluate the condition of that ***else if*** statement. If it evaluates to ***true***, the ***else if*** block will be executed and the remaining ***else if*** and ***else blocks*** (if present) will be ignored; if it evaluates to ***false***, the control will go to the next ***else if*** or ***else*** statements if there are any. You can have as many ***else if*** statements as you want. The general syntax is as follows:

```
if ( <condition 1>)
      {
            //This block will be executed if <condition
1> is true.
      }
else if ( <condition 2> )
{
            //This block will be executed if <condition
            1> is false <condition 2> is true.
            <statements…>
      }
      else if ( <condition 3> )
      {
            //This block will be executed if <condition
            1>    and    <condition    2>    are    false    and
            <condition 3> is true.
            <statements…>
      }
      else
      {
            //This block will be executed if <condition
            1>,   <condition   2>   and   <condition   3>   are
            false.
      }
```

Note: If there is only one statement inside an if, else if or else block, there is no need to specify the block inside curly brackets.

To demonstrate the if – else if – else construct, let us write a Java program to accept an integer from the user and check if it is positive, negative or zero. Here is the code:

```
import java.util.*;

public class IfElseDemo
{
```

```
    public static void main ( String [] args )
    {
        //Declare and initialize Scanner object scanobj
        Scanner scanobj = new Scanner( System.in );
        //Ask the user to enter a number
        System.out.println("\nEnter a number: ");
        //Read user input as integer
        int number = scanobj.nextInt();
        //Check if the number is +ve
        if ( number > 0 )
            System.out.println("\nThe number " + number + " is positive.\n");
        //Check if the number is -ve
        else if ( number < 0 )
            System.out.println("\nThe number " + number + " is negative.\n");
        //If the number is neither positive nor negative, means it is zero
        else
            System.out.println("\nThe number " + number + " is zero.\n");
    }
}
```

Output:

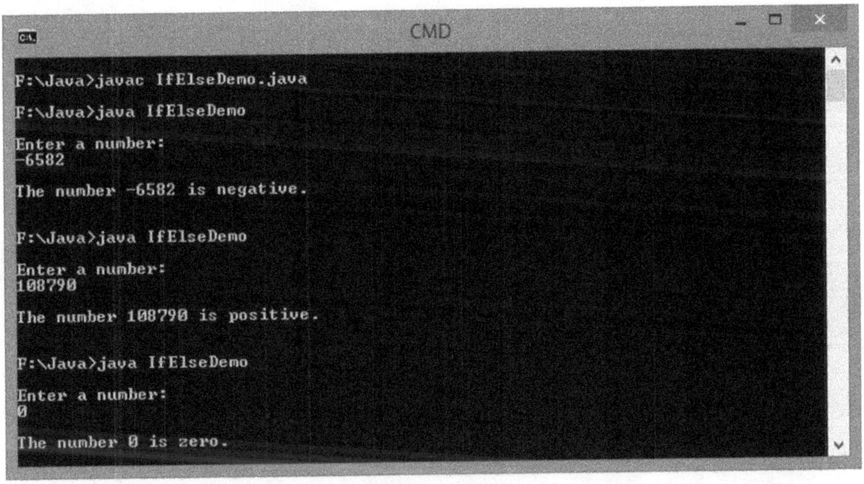

```
CMD

F:\Java>javac IfElseDemo.java

F:\Java>java IfElseDemo

Enter a number:
-6582

The number -6582 is negative.

F:\Java>java IfElseDemo

Enter a number:
108790

The number 108790 is positive.

F:\Java>java IfElseDemo

Enter a number:
0

The number 0 is zero.
```

The program has been executed thrice to demonstrate that we are successfully checking for positive, negative and zero. An important thing to note here is – we are compiling the program only once and executing thrice. This is because we are not using any hardcoded data and always asking the user to enter a number.

8.1.2 switch-case Construct

During decision making, evaluation of an expression can lead to multiple outcomes. One way to take care of each outcome is to have a long list of ***if, else if*** and nested ***if, else if, else*** statements; it will work perfectly fine. But there is a cleaner, efficient and more organized way to do this using the ***switch-case*** construct. The general syntax of a ***switch-case*** construct is:

```
switch (<expression>)
{
        case <constant expression 1>:
                //Statements to be executed if this case is matched.
        case <constant expression 1>:
                //Statements to be executed if this case is matched.
        ... ...
        ... ...
        ... ...
        case <constant expression N>:
                //Statements to be executed if this case is matched.
        default:
                //Statements to be executed if no case is matched.
}
```

A switch statement must be supplied with an expression which is evaluated and a decision is made. The supplied expression is denoted by ***<expression>*** field in the above code snippet. This expression need not necessarily be a Boolean expression. Each outcome that this expression can evaluate to is known as a ***case***. When the ***<expression>*** is evaluated, the program looks for the matching constant expression supplied with each of the cases present inside the switch block. If a match is found, that particular ***case block*** is executed. If no match is found, the program executes the ***default case*** block if present. This process is known as ***testing for cases***. Once a matching case is found, all the statements after that case block are executed until a ***break;*** statement is encountered. A ***break;*** statement is used to take the control out of a switch block. It is also possible to nest switch blocks. In case of nested switch blocks, a break statement encountered in the inner switch block will only bring the control out of that particular block and not from the whole nested switch arrangement.

The working of a switch case construct can be explained in a better way with the help of an example. Let us write a program where in we will prompt the user to enter a number and check if it is odd or even.

```
import java.util.*;

public class SwitchDemo
{
   public static void main ( String [] args )
   {
          //Declare  and  initialize  Scanner  object
scanobj
          Scanner scanobj = new Scanner( System.in );
          //Ask the user to enter a number
          System.out.println("\nEnter a number: ");
          //Read user input as integer
          int number = scanobj.nextInt();
```

```
            //Test for cases using switch
            switch ( number % 2 )
            {
                  //If number % 2 == 0, the number is
even
                  case 0:
                        System.out.println("\nThe
number " + number + " is even.\n");
                        break;
                  //If number % 2 == 1, the number is
odd
                  case 1:
                        System.out.println("\nThe
number " + number + " is odd.\n");
                        break;
            }
      }
   }
```

Output:

```
CMD
F:\Java>javac SwitchDemo.java

F:\Java>java SwitchDemo

Enter a number:
5

The number 5 is odd.

F:\Java>java SwitchDemo

Enter a number:
36

The number 36 is even.

F:\Java>_
```

8.2 Loops

Loops are used to execute a block of code over and over again until a specific condition is met. Each instance of a loop block execution is known as an ***iteration***. Java offers three loops – ***while loop, do while loop and for loop***.

8.2.1 while Loop

Syntax for using while loop is as follows:

```
while (<condition>)
{
        //Statements...
}
```

A while loop should be supplied with a condition denoted by the ***<condition>*** field in the above snippet. The ***<condition>*** should be a Boolean expression and can evaluate to either ***true*** or ***false***. If the ***<condition>*** evaluates to ***true***, the statements inside the ***while block*** are executed in a sequential order. Once the execution reaches the end of the block, the specified condition is checked again and if it evaluates to ***true***, the block is executed again. This process goes on until the specified condition evaluates to ***false***. Here is a snippet to display numbers from 1 to 10 on the screen using a while loop:

```
//Initialize an integer variable to 1
int number = 1;
//Loop until number is less than or equal to 10
while ( number <= 10 )
{
        //Display number
        System.out.println ( number );
        //Increment number
        number ++;
}
```

8.2.2 do-while Loop

Syntax for using do-while loop is as follows:

```
do
{
        //Statements...
} while (<condition>);
```

The ***do while*** loop and ***while*** loops work in a similar fashion; however, in a ***do while*** loop, instead of checking the specified condition at the beginning, it is checked at the end of the loop block. That is, when the program encounters a do-while block, the statements inside it are immediately executed and then the condition is checked. This means, the statements under a ***do-while*** loop will be executed at least once even if the specified condition evaluates to ***false.***

Here is a snippet to display numbers from 1 to 10 on the screen using a do-while loop:

```
//Initialize an integer variable to 1
int number = 1;
do
{
        //Display number
        System.out.println ( number );
        //Increment number
        number ++;
        //Loop until number is less than or equal to
10
} while ( number <= 10 );
```

Let us write a program to accept an integer from the user; reverse it using ***while*** loop and calculate the sum of all digits using ***do while*** loop. To do both these things, we need to extract the digits of a given number one by one. If we take ***modulus-10***

(number % 10) of a number, it will be divided by 10 and the remainder will be returned which will be the last digit (present at one's place). Once we have the last digit, we need to discard it from the number so that we can extract the next digit. This can be done by dividing the number by 10. We have seen in ***Section 6.1*** that when an integer is divided by another integer, the quotient will be an integer. For example, ***12345 / 10*** will result in ***1234***; this is exactly what we need here. The code is as follows:

```
import java.util.*;

public class SumAndReverse
{
   public static void main ( String [] args )
   {
         //Declare some variables
         int number, x, sum = 0, reverse = 0;
         //Declare and initialize Scanner object
scanobj
         Scanner scanobj = new Scanner( System.in );
         //Ask the user to enter a number
         System.out.println("\nEnter a number: ");
         //Read user input as integer
         number = scanobj.nextInt();
         //Copy number to x as we will need it later
         x = number ;
         //Calculate the sum of digits
         //Loop while number (x) is not equal to 0
         while ( x != 0 )
         {
               //Add one's digit to sum
               sum = sum + ( x % 10 ) ;
               //Discard one's place digit
               x = x / 10 ;
         }
         //We have lost the contents of x, set it
again
         x = number ;
         //Calculate the reverse
         //Loop while number (x) is not equal to 0
         do
```

```
            {
                    //Multiply 10 to reverse to take it to
the next place
                    //Add one's digit to reverse
                    reverse = (reverse * 10 ) + ( x % 10
) ;

                    //Discard one's plcae digit
                    x = x / 10 ;
            } while ( x != 0 );
            //Display everything
            System.out.println("\nNumber: " + number +
                                            "\nSum    of
digits: " + sum +
                                            "\nReverse: "
+ reverse );
        }
    }
```

Output:

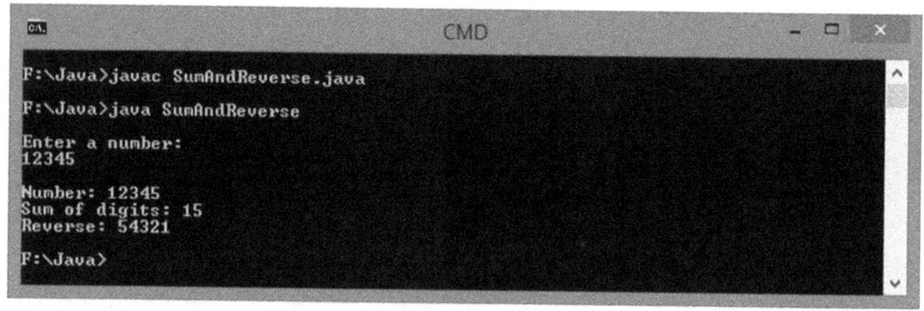

8.3.3 for Loop

Syntax for using for loop is as follows:

```
    for ( <loop variable initialization> ; <condition>
; <expression> )
    {
            <statements...>
    }
```

The ***for loop*** is a well-structured loop having more features that the ***while*** and ***do while*** loops. It allows you to use a special loop variable for iterating purpose. Until the specified ***<condition>*** evaluates to ***true***, the loop will go on executing. The ***<expression>*** can contain any mathematical expression, this field is usually used to ***increment*** or ***decrement*** the loop variable. In case of ***while*** or ***do while loops***, the loop variable had to be incremented/ decremented somewhere inside the block. As seen from the syntax of the for loop, this can be done in the ***for*** statement itself.

Here is a snippet to display numbers from 1 to 10 on the screen using a ***for loop***:

```
//Declare an integer variable
int number;
for ( number = 1 ; number <= 10 ; number ++)
{
        //Display number
        System.out.println ( number );
}
```

Let us write a Java program to accept an integer from the user and calculate its ***factorial*** using a for loop. A factorial of a number ***n*** is mathematically denoted by ***n!*** where ***n! = n x (n - 1) x (n - 2) x ...... x 1***. For example, ***6! = 6 x 5 x 4 x 3 x 2 x 1 = 720***. The expression ***n!*** can also be written as ***n! = n x (n - 1)!*** . Factorial of 0 is 1. Here is the program:

```
import java.util.*;

public class Factorial
{
   public static void main ( String [] args )
   {
        //Declare some variables
        int number, factorial = 1;
```

```
            //Declare and initialize Scanner object scanobj
            Scanner scanobj = new Scanner( System.in );
            //Ask the user to enter a number
            System.out.println("\nEnter a number: ");
            //Read user input as integer
            number = scanobj.nextInt();
            //Loop from 1 to number using a for loop
            //Declare and use a loop variable i
            for ( int i = 1 ; i <= number ; i++ )
                  factorial = factorial * i ;
            //Display everything
            System.out.println("\nNumber: " + number +
                                                "\nFactorial: " + factorial);
      }
}
```

Output:

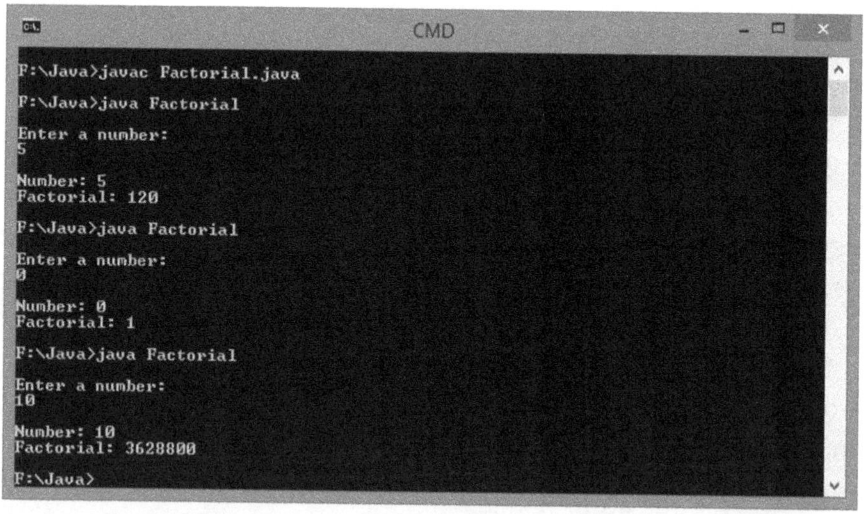

```
CMD
F:\Java>javac Factorial.java

F:\Java>java Factorial

Enter a number:
5

Number: 5
Factorial: 120

F:\Java>java Factorial

Enter a number:
0

Number: 0
Factorial: 1

F:\Java>java Factorial

Enter a number:
10

Number: 10
Factorial: 3628800

F:\Java>
```

Note: If there is only one statement inside the loop block, there is no need to enclose the loop block inside curly brackets.

8.3.4 Control Statements

Java offers two control statements – ***break;*** and ***continue;*** When the program execution finds a ***break;*** statement, the execution control comes out of the loop and when a ***continue;*** statement is encountered, the execution control will go to the beginning of the loop thereby ignoring all the statements after the ***continue;*** statement. In case of a ***for*** loop, the ***continue*** statement takes the execution to the beginning of the loop and executes the ***<expression>***, thereby incrementing/decrementing the loop variable.

9. Functions

A function, also known as a method is a block of code used to perform a specific task. So far, we have already come across pre-defined functions such as ***println ( )*** used to display data on the screen and ***nextInt ( )*** to read an integer from the user. In this section, we will learn how to define our own functions and use them to carry out tasks of our choice. What you need to understand in this topic is – ***function definition*** and ***function call***.

9.1 Function Definition

A function can be defined in the main class (public) or you can have a non-public class and define function within that class. We will only learn about declaring functions inside the main class. The general syntax for declaring a function is:

```
<access specifier> <return type> <function name> ( <parameter> )
{
    //Function Body
    //Statements
}
```

The access specifier can be ***default*** or ***public***; since we are declaring this function inside the main class, we need to make this function a ***static*** one as it should be common throughout the class. A function can perform its task and optionally return a value back to the calling function. The ***<return type>*** field specifies the type of data the function returns. If a function returns a value, there must be a mandatory ***return <value/variable>;*** statement at the end of the function body. If a function does not return any value, the return type should be ***void***. The ***<parameters>*** field is a list of variables, each separated by a comma. These are used to accept data from the calling function. Here are a few examples:

```
//A function that does not return anything, does not have any parameters
static void display ( )
{
        System.out.println("Inside a function!");
}
//A function that does not return anything, has two parameters, displays them
static void displaydata ( int a, int b )
{
        System.out.println("a = " + a + " b = " + b );
}
//A function that accepts 3 double values and returns their sum as double
static double add ( double x, double y, double z )
{
        double sum = x + y + z ;
        //Mandatory return statement as the return type is double.
        return sum;
}
```

9.2 Function Call

When a function is defined, that block of code is simply sitting idle. You need to activate that function by calling it. To call a function, the following syntax is used:

```
<function name> ( <parameters> );
```

If a function is returning a value, a variable is required to receive it. In such a case, the syntax would be:

```
<variable> = <function name> ( <parameters> );
```

If you do not receive the returned value in a variable, the returned value will be lost.

There are 3 examples of function definition in ***Section 9.1***. Let us see how to call them:

```
//Call static void display ( ) as follows:
display ( ) ;
//Call static void displaydata ( int a, int b ) as follows
//10 and 20 are used as an example, could be any other integer value.
displaydata ( 10, 20 );
//Call static double add ( double x, double y, double z ) as follows:
//549.5, 435.75, 1334.535 are used as an example, could be any other double value.
//A variable is needed to receive the returned data.
double sum = add ( 549.5, 435.75, 1334.535);
```

Note: When parameters are passed to a function, they are also known as arguments. The number and type of parameters in the function definition should match the argument list when a call is made to that function and should also be in the exact order.

You may now recall ***Section 7*** where we learned about accepting user input using the functions of the ***Scanner class***. Having the knowledge of functions will make a lot more sense when using pre-defined functions.

Let us write a Java program to write different kinds of functions and call them from the main method.

```
public class FunctionDemo
{
    //A function that does not accept any parameters
and
    //does not return any value
    static void SimpleFunction ()
    {
        System.out.println("\nInside SimpleFunction
( )");
    }
    //A function that accepts 2 integers and
    //does not return any value
    static void DisplayProduct (int a, int b)
    {
        System.out.println("\nInside DisplayProduct
(int a, int b)");
        System.out.println("\na = " + a + " b = " +
                            b + " a x b =
" + (a * b) );
    }
    //A function that accepts 3 double values and
    //returns the sum as double
    //Hence it has a return type of double
    static double Add (double a, double b, double c)
    {
        System.out.println("\nInside double Add
(double a, double b, double c)");
        return (a + b + c);
    }
    public static void main ( String [] args )
    {
        System.out.println("\nInside public static
void main ( String [] args )");
        //Call SimplFunction()
        SimpleFunction();
        //Call DisplayProduct, pass some arguments
        DisplayProduct(9854, 100);
        //Call Add(), pass some arguments
```

```
            double  sum  =  Add  (35425.765,  524.75,
4604.0575);
            System.out.println("\nInside  public  static
void main ( String [] args )" +
                                    "\nsum  =  "  +
sum);
        }
    }
```

Output:

```
CMD
F:\Java>javac FunctionDemo.java
F:\Java>java FunctionDemo
Inside public static void main ( String [] args )
Inside SimpleFunction ( )
Inside DisplayProduct (int a, int b)
a = 9854 b = 100 a x b = 985400
Inside double Add (double a, double b, double c)
Inside public static void main ( String [] args )
sum = 40554.5725
F:\Java>_
```

Java supports ***Function Overloading*** which is a concept of ***polymorphism*** where in you can have multiple functions having the same name carrying out different tasks. Without proper understanding of OOP concepts, function overloading can be confusing and hence it is not covered. While defining your own functions, make sure that the function name is unique within the class.

10. Arrays

An array is a collection of similar items. Each item is known as an element. You can have arrays of any data type, including custom data types. The position of an element in the array is known as an index. Array index starts at 0 and goes up to ***(size – 1)***. For example, if you had an array of 5 elements, the index would go from 0 to 4. The first element would be present at index 0 and the last element would be present at index 4. The syntax of declaring arrays is:

```
<data type> <array variable>[ ];
    //OR
    <data type>[ ] <array variable>;
Eg:
int numbers [ ];
float [ ] values;
String [ ] names;
```

Once an array is declared, it needs to be ***initiated*** using the ***new*** keyword as follows:

```
<array variable> = new <data type>[ <array size> ];
```

Alternatively, this can be done while declaration itself as follows:

```
<data type>[ ] <array variable> = new <data type>[
<array size> ];
//OR
<data type> <array variable> [ ] = new <data type>[
<array size> ];
Eg:
      int numbers [ ] = new int [10];
      String [ ] names;
      names = new String [5];
```

You can even ***declare, initiate and initialize*** an array all in one statement as follows:

```
<data type>[ ] <array variable> = new <data type> [
] { <value 1>, … <value n>}
Eg:
int[] numbers = new int[ ] { 1, 2, 3, 4, 5 };
```

There is no need to specify the size when initializing an array, it will automatically be taken.

You can access each element of an array using the ***access operator ([ ])***. The syntax is:

```
<array variable> [ <index> ]
```

Consider the following array of integers:

```
int [ ] num = new int [ ] {65, 89, 12, 53, 36};
```

This is what it is going to look like in the memory:

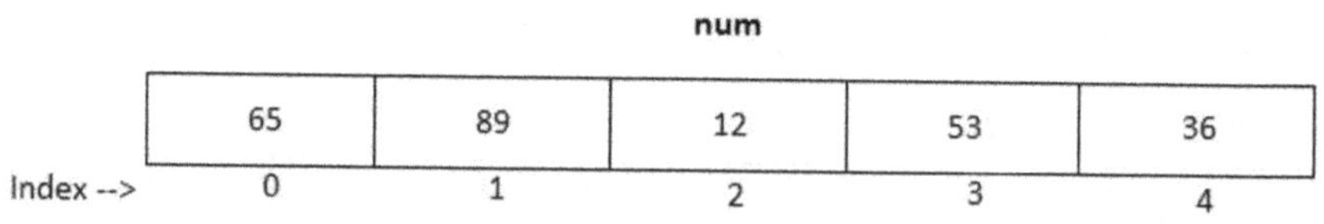

num

	65	89	12	53	36
Index -->	0	1	2	3	4

While accessing using array index:

```
num [ 0 ] will be 65
num [ 1 ] will be 89
num [ 2 ] will be 12
num [ 3 ] will be 53
num [ 4 ] will be 36
```

Let us write a Java program to declare, initiate and initialize a double array of 5 values. Calculate sum and average of all the elements of that array. Here is the program:

```
public class ArraysDemo
{
   public static void main ( String [] args )
   {
         //Declare, initiate and initialize a double
array
         double data [ ] = new double [ ] { 36.58,
45.05, 98.33, 50.92, 99.67 };
         //Display elements
         for ( int i = 0 ; i < 5 ; i ++)
               System.out.println ("Index: " + i + "
Value: " + data [i]);
         //Calculate Sum of all Elements and the
average;
         double sum = 0 , average;
         for ( int i = 0 ; i < 5 ; i ++)
               sum += data [i] ;
         average = sum / 5 ;
         //Display sum and average
         System.out.println ("Sum: " + sum + "
Average: " + average);
   }
}
```

Output:

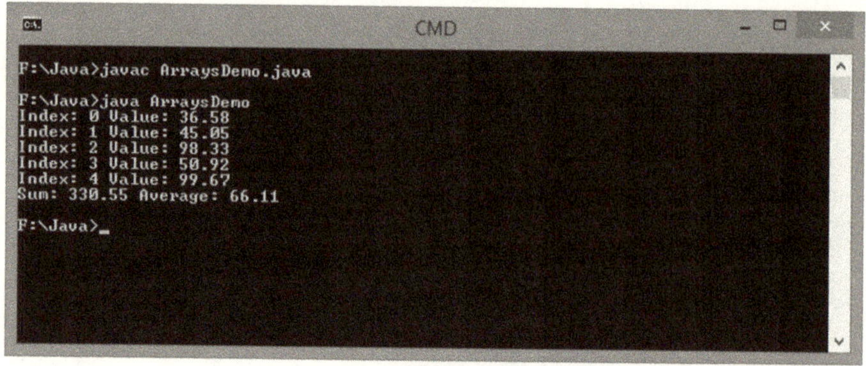

Note 1: Array index can only be an integer.

Note 2: If index exceeds (size – 1), it will result in an error.

11. Strings

A string is a sequence of characters. In Java, ***String*** is an object-type data type and not a primitive one. We have already seen how to declare and use strings, let us go through it again. Syntax for string declaration:

```
String <variable name>;
```

You can initialize a string just as you would initialize any other variable. For example:

```
String name = "Alice", city = "London";
```

You can even have an array of strings as follows:

```
String [ ] <variable>;
```

Declaration, initiation and initialization of ***String*** arrays is the same as discussed in the ***Arrays*** section.

You can concatenate strings as follows:

```
<concatenated string> = <string 1> + <string 2> + …
<string n>;
Eg:
String message, s = "Hello";
message = s + "World";
```

In the above example, there are two variables ***message*** and ***s*** of ***String*** type. The statement *message = s + "World";* will append the string ***"World"*** to the contents of ***s*** and save it in ***message***. Hence, message will now hold ***"HelloWorld".*** There are plenty of built in functions to work with strings, covering all of those is beyond the scope of this book. Following are a few useful ones:

char charAt(int index)

Returns the character at the specified index.

boolean endsWith(String suffix)

Checks if this string ends with the given suffix.

int indexOf(int ch/String str)

Returns the index of the first occurrence of the given character or string.

int lastIndexOf(int ch/String str)

Returns the index of the last occurrence of the given character or string.

int length()

Returns the length of the string.

String replace(char oldChar, char newChar)

Replaces all occurrences of oldChar with newChar and returns the new string.

String substring(int beginIndex)

Returns a new string starting from beginIndex.

String toLowerCase()

Converts all of the characters in this String to lower case.

String toUpperCase()

Converts all of the characters in this String to upper case.

Let us write a Java program to accept a string as user input and perform various operations using some of this functions:

```
import java.util.*;

public class StringDemo
{
   public static void main ( String [] args )
   {
         //Declare and initialize Scanner object scanobj
         Scanner scanobj = new Scanner( System.in );
         //Ask the user to enter a String
         System.out.println("\nEnter a String: ");
         //Read user input as integer
         String str = scanobj.nextLine();
         //Find the length
         int length = str.length();
         //Find the first character
         char first = str.charAt(0);
         //Find the last character
         char last = str.charAt(length - 1);
         //Convert to upper case
         String upper = str.toUpperCase();
         //Convert to lower case
         String lower = str.toLowerCase();
         //Display Everything
         System.out.println("\n\nInput: " + str +
                            "\nLength: " + length +
                            "\nFirst Character: " + first +
                            "\nLast Character: " + last +
                            "\nUpper Case: " + upper +
                            "\nLower Case: " + lower );
   }
}
```

Output:

```
CMD

F:\Java>javac StringDemo.java

F:\Java>java StringDemo

Enter a String:
Hello, this is the StringDemo Program


Input: Hello, this is the StringDemo Program
Length: 37
First Character: H
Last Character: m
Upper Case: HELLO, THIS IS THE STRINGDEMO PROGRAM
Lower Case: hello, this is the stringdemo program

F:\Java>
```

These are only a handful of built-in functions. I strongly recommend going through the Java documents to learn about other built-in functions.

12. Final Words

Java is one of the most widely used languages out there and has been around for quite a long time. With Java, you can do almost anything; be it desktop software development, web development, mobile application development, etc.

I have covered the very basics of Java, just enough to get started. If you liked your journey with this programming language so far, I strongly recommend learning object oriented programming in Java and other advanced concepts. Once you have a hold over OOP, you will be able to learn Android application development or web development with ease.

Having good knowledge of Java will help you learn other programming languages such as C#, Python, etc.

Hope you have learned something of value from this book.

Good Luck & Happy Coding!

If you enjoyed this book as much as I've enjoyed writing it, you can subscribe* to my email list for exclusive content and sneak peaks of my future books.

Go to the link below:

http://eepurl.com/du_L4n

OR

Use the QR Code:

(*Must be 13 years or older to subscribe)

www.ingramcontent.com/pod-product-compliance
Lightning Source LLC
Chambersburg PA
CBHW031246050326
40690CB00007B/969

* 9 7 8 1 7 9 3 9 8 2 8 3 4 *